guiding
your
teenagers

homebuilders

PARENTING SERIES®

guiding
your
teenagers

by
dennis & barbara
rainey

FAMILYLIFE®

Little Rock, Arkansas

GUIDING YOUR TEENAGERS
FamilyLife Publishing®
5800 Ranch Drive
Little Rock, Arkansas 72223
1-800-FL-TODAY • FamilyLife.com
FLTI, d/b/a FamilyLife®, is a ministry of Campus Crusade for Christ International®

ISBN: 978-1-60200-350-7

Design: Brand Navigation, LLC

Cover image: Masterfile Corporation

Printed in the United States of America

15 14 13 12 11   2 3 4 5 6

FAMILYLIFE®

Unless the LORD builds the house,
those who build it labor in vain.

PSALM 127:1

welcome to homebuilders

When we bring a new life into the world, we burst with pride and joy... but are often unprepared to raise that child to become a mature, responsible adult.

In response to this need, FamilyLife has developed the HomeBuilders Parenting Series with several goals in mind: (1) to encourage you and help you not to feel overwhelmed by the responsibilities of parenting, (2) to help you develop a practical and biblical plan for parenting, (3) to enhance and strengthen your teamwork as a couple, (4) to help you connect with other parents so you can encourage and help one another, and (5) to help you strengthen your relationship with God.

You will notice as you proceed through this study that the Bible is cited as the authority on issues of life, marriage, and parenting. The Bible is God's Word—his blueprint for building a godly home and for dealing with the practical issues of living. Although written nearly two thousand years ago, Scripture still speaks clearly and powerfully about the concerns we face in our families.

A Special Word to Single Parents

Although the primary audience for this study is married couples, we recognize that single parents can also benefit from the experience. If you are a single parent, you will find that while some of the language may not be directed to your circumstances, the teaching and principles are highly applicable and can help you develop a solid, workable plan for your family.

Do we really need to be part of a group? Couldn't we just go through this study as a couple?

While you could work through the study as a couple, you would miss the opportunity to connect with friends and to learn from one another's experiences. You will find that the questions in each session not only help you grow closer to your spouse, but they also create an environment of warmth and fellowship with other couples as you study together.

What does it take to lead a HomeBuilders group?

Leading a group is much easier than you may think, because the leader is simply a facilitator who guides the participants through the discussion questions. You are not teaching the material but are helping the couples discover and apply biblical truths. The special dynamic of a HomeBuilders group is that couples teach themselves.

The study guide you're holding has all the information and guidance you need to participate in or lead a HomeBuilders group. You'll find leader's notes in the back of the guide, and additional helps are posted online at FamilyLife.com/Resources.

What is the typical schedule?

Most studies in the HomeBuilders Parenting Series are six to eight weeks long, indicated by the number of sessions in the guide. The sessions are designed to take sixty minutes in the group with a project for the couples to complete between sessions.

Isn't it risky to talk about your family in a group?

The group setting should be enjoyable and informative—and nonthreatening. **THREE SIMPLE GROUND RULES** will help ensure that everyone feels comfortable and gets the most out of the experience:

1. Share nothing that will embarrass your spouse or violate the trust of your children.
2. You may pass on any question you do not want to answer.
3. If possible, as a couple complete the HomeBuilders project between group sessions.

What other help does FamilyLife offer?

Our list of marriage and family resources continues to grow. Visit FamilyLife.com to learn more about our:

- Weekend to Remember® getaway, The Art of Marriage, and other events;
- slate of radio broadcasts, including the nationally syndicated *FamilyLife Today*®, *Real FamilyLife with Dennis Rainey*®, and *FamilyLife This Week*®;
- multimedia resources for small groups, churches, and community networking;
- interactive products for parents, couples, small-group leaders, and one-to-one mentors; and
- assortment of blogs, forums, and other online connections.

on guiding your teenagers

Teenagers are vulnerable. They're just a few years or months from facing adult-sized life with child-sized experience. As a parent, you're right to be concerned. You know how challenging life can be, and you have a good idea how your teens are likely to be tested. But if you try to step in and help them prepare for what's ahead, they might resist and push you away.

Parenting through the teen years requires great balance and agility. At any moment and with very little notice, you shift from coach to spectator as your child wants your guidance one day and your detachment the next. Your relationship changes as he or she becomes more independent. But in reality, your teen needs you as much as ever.

We understand that teenagers can be puzzling to parents, and it's sometimes easy to think that you've done all you can do. But please don't abandon your post. Even as you're "letting them go," you still have a job to do. Your work isn't finished.

We've developed this study with the desire to help parents guide their children through the maze of adolescence and into lives of godly purpose. May you all learn and grow through this process.

—Dennis & Barbara Rainey

contents

1
The Traps of
Adolescence

Equipping your teenage children to avoid the traps of adolescence requires that you stay relationally connected with them.

Growing Up Is Hard to Do

Introduce yourself and tell the group the names and ages of your children. Then answer one or two of the following questions:

- Think back to the years when you began to move from childhood into your teen years. What were some of the ways you began to change as you went through those years?
- As a sixteen-year-old, what was one of your biggest priorities or problems?

- Does your teenager remind you of yourself at that age? In what way(s)?
- What do you hope to gain from this study?

blueprints

Case Study

Read the following case study aloud, using volunteer readers for each of the three parts:

Mike and Lori are having a conversation about their thirteen-year-old daughter, Lauren.

Mike: I guess Lauren is growing up faster than I want.

Lori: What do you mean?

Mike: She doesn't seem to want to do anything with me anymore. I just asked if she wanted to go get some doughnuts—like we have every Saturday morning ever since she was two years old. Now she doesn't seem to care about it.

Lori: I know what you mean. She used to run up and hug me whenever she saw me at her school. Now she acts like she's embarrassed to see me.

Mike: I guess I knew this was coming, but I didn't realize it would start so soon.

Lauren enters the room.

Lauren: I'm going to the mall this afternoon with Alyssa.

Lori: Really? I don't remember any discussion about going to the mall.

Lauren: It's just the mall, Mom. I didn't realize I had to ask permission for everything I do.

Lori: And how were you planning to get there?

Lauren: Alyssa's brother is going to take us, and we were going to have you pick us up.

Mike: Hold on a minute. I'm not so sure I like the idea of you two going to the mall without a parent. I'm not sure it's safe for girls your age.

Lauren: But Dad, all our friends do it. We're going to meet them there.

Mike: Let me talk to your mother about it, and we'll decide.

Lauren: Why are you always so strict? None of the other kids' parents seem to have a problem with this.

Mike: Your mother and I will discuss it, and we'll get back to you.

Lauren: Well, hurry up. I've got to call Alyssa to let her know.

Lauren exits in a huff.

Lori: Is this how we acted with our parents when we were that age?

1. How can you relate to the situation Mike and Lori face with their daughter? In what ways has your child been showing a greater desire for independence?

2. What advice would you give Mike and Lori?

Drifting Apart

We like to call the time period before children enter adolescence the "golden years." These are the years (ages six to eleven) when parenting seems easier for many. Your children actually listen to you and enjoy your company. Then as they approach and enter adolescence, their growing need for independence often leads them to think they no longer need much input from parents or other adults. Instead, they rely on their peers. Popular media and advertising often encourage this type of thinking, portraying parents as old-fashioned and restrictive, while teenagers are shown as being capable of making wise decisions.

3. Read Proverbs 22:15. What do you think this verse means when it says that "folly is bound up in the heart of a child"? In what ways do teenagers sometimes demonstrate folly?

Keeping the Connection

As God was creating the nation of Israel, the family was established as one of the key foundations for society. Parents were given the responsibility to tell their children about God and teach each succeeding generation about the Bible.

4. Read through the instructions given to parents in Deuteronomy 6:1–9. What does this passage say about

    - the personal character that parents should demonstrate?

    - the type of relationship parents should have with their children in order to teach them about God and the Bible?

Involvement can mean different things to different parents. Some parents think they're involved with their adolescent children because they eat dinner together several nights a week or attend all their basketball or volleyball games. If you want to help your child make wise choices during adolescence, you'll need to be committed to a higher level of involvement than that. Your children may not always welcome this type of involvement, and it may feel uncomfortable at times, but it's essential.

5. List some ways you can stay connected and involved with your adolescent children, even when they display little interest in your involvement. What has worked for you?

 HomeBuilders Principle: To help your children grow up to walk with God, you need to take the initiative to remain involved during their adolescent years.

Recognizing the Traps

During their teenage years, children face a lot of different pressures and problems that we like to call the "traps of adolescence." These are the snares that lure a teenager into making foolish choices. Many of us were caught by some of these traps ourselves when we were teenagers.

For example, one obvious trap is sex. We live in a culture that encourages young people to experiment with sex at a very early age.

6. What are some other traps that threaten teenagers today?

Walking in the Truth

One of the reasons teenagers are so easily caught in the traps of adolescence is that many have only a vague set of beliefs to guide their behavior and their choices. Even teens who call themselves Christians often don't know what they believe and don't understand how the truth of the Bible can influence their daily lives.

7. Read 3 John 3–4. What do you think it means for children to be "walking in the truth," and why is this important? How does walking in the truth differ from walking in lies?

A Legacy of Biblical Convictions

One of the keys to helping teenagers learn to walk in the truth is for you to pass on biblical convictions that will help them make good choices. What is a conviction? We like the definition author Josh McDowell presents in his book *Beyond Belief to Convictions*.

Having a conviction, he writes, "is being so thoroughly convinced that something is absolutely true that you take a stand for it regardless of the consequences."

That is what your children need—a set of biblical convictions that will help them negotiate the traps of adolescence. One reason many parents don't pass on biblical convictions to their children is they haven't clarified their own convictions.

Answer question 8 with your spouse. After answering, you may want to share an appropriate insight or discovery with the group.

8. Take a minute to look over the following list of various traps of adolescence. Select one of these for which you have particularly strong convictions; then write a sentence that expresses one of your convictions and share it with your spouse.

- **Peer pressure**—the influence peers have in one's life (for example: "Bad company corrupts good character")
- **Sex**—biblical standards for purity before marriage
- **Dating**—guidelines for spending time with the opposite sex
- **Media**—standards on what to watch, read, or listen to, and how much time to devote to media
- **Appearance**—appropriate dress and grooming for different occasions
- **Attitude**—maintaining a proper perspective on yourself, your parents, and authority figures
- **Substance abuse**—using alcohol, drugs, and other potentially harmful substances

- **Pornography**—exposing yourself to images that degrade God's standards on sex

9. Why is it important for your children to know your convictions and to see you model them?

 HomeBuilders Principle: Now is the time to clarify and begin modeling your biblical convictions on real-life issues your teenager will face.

Parent to Parent

During the next five sessions, we'll examine five of the hottest issues you'll face with your teenagers:

- Peer pressure
- Sex
- Dating
- Media
- Substance abuse

In each session we'll talk about why each trap is particularly dangerous, and we'll challenge you with some biblical convictions to build into your teenagers. For now we'll leave you with some insights we've gleaned from our experience:

1. Never underestimate the capacity of your teenagers to make foolish choices.
2. Staying involved in the life of your teenagers may be the most demanding and courageous commitment you can make as a parent.
3. Involvement means not losing heart when you don't see immediate results.
4. Never assume that your teenagers will learn all they need to walk in the truth through the influence of church, youth group, or a Christian school. Your role is critical.
5. Your example will speak louder than your words.

make a date

Set a time for you and your spouse to complete the HomeBuilders project together before the next group meeting. You will be asked at the next session to share an insight or experience from the project.

date _____ time _____

location _____

homebuilders project

On Your Own

1. In what ways were you challenged by the first session of this study?

2. What expectations do you have for this study?

3. In the group discussion, we talked about the importance of determining your convictions on the key issues your child will face as a teenager. Following is a list of a number of these issues. Review the list and evaluate how well you think you've developed convictions in each of these areas. Rate yourself with one of two marks:

    - Y (for yes) if you can articulate a clear conviction for each issue
    - N (for no) if you cannot

      Personal Convictions Development
      Peer pressure __
      Biblical view of sex __
      Dating guidelines __

Media consumption __

Dealing with anger __

Appearance __

Deceit __

Substance abuse __

Pornography __

Lordship of Christ __

Other: _____ __

Other: _____ __

Using the same marks, also rate yourself on how you're doing in shaping your child's convictions in these areas. Remember that for something to be a conviction, you must think it's so true that you'll take a stand for it regardless of the consequences.

Shaping of Child's Convictions
Peer pressure __

Biblical view of sex __

Dating guidelines __

Media consumption __

Dealing with anger __

Appearance __

Deceit __

Substance abuse __

Pornography __

Lordship of Christ __

Other: _____ __

Other: _____ __

4. In which area do you most need to develop stronger convictions? In which area do you most need to shape convictions in your teen (or teens)?

With Your Spouse

1. Share your responses to the questions you answered on your own.

2. Discuss what you're currently doing to provide your children with biblical and spiritual instruction.

3. In addition to the things you're already doing, what else should you consider doing to help develop convictions in your children?

4. Close in prayer, asking God for wisdom as you seek to help guide your teen through the traps of adolescence.

Be sure to check out the related Parent-Teen Interactions beginning on page 79.

2

Peer
Pressure

Your involvement in your teenager's life will help
him or her exercise wisdom in choosing friends
and resisting unhealthy influences from peers.

warm-up

Avoiding the Traps

For this exercise you'll need a blindfold, six to eight sheets of
paper, some tape, and six to eight objects to place on the floor.
You can use chairs, books, boxes, lamps—anything you want. On
each sheet of paper, write the name of one of the following "traps"
of adolescence:

- Sex
- Substance abuse
- Media
- Pornography

- Dating
- Peer pressure
- Attitude
- Appearance

Tape the sheets of paper to the different objects. Blindfold one person and place him or her at one end of the room. Then situate the objects in the room in such a way that it's impossible to walk in a straight line from one end of the room to the other without running into one of the traps.

Have a volunteer try to walk blindfolded from one end of the room to the other without touching any of the objects. As the blindfolded volunteer attempts to navigate this mini obstacle course, everyone should offer advice—loudly and simultaneously!

After the volunteer attempts to negotiate the obstacle course this way, try again. This time, one person should act as a guide— standing next to the blindfolded person and coaching him or her through the obstacle course while the group is silent.

When finished, discuss these questions:

- How would you compare this exercise to the world in which teens live?

- What does this exercise teach us about how the traps of adolescence can be avoided?

Project Report

Share one thing you learned from the HomeBuilders project from the previous session.

The Effects of Peer Pressure

Peer pressure isn't just an issue for teenagers. How often do you compare what you have with what others have? Are you ever tempted to buy certain brands of cars or clothes because that's what your friends prefer? Are you ever hesitant to express your opinion because others may not agree?

Peer pressure is inescapable. But for teenagers it's an especially dangerous trap.

1. In high school, what person or group had the most influence on you? What effect did your peer group have on the kind of choices you made? If you can, give an example.

2. In what ways have you seen your child influenced by peers recently—for good or for bad?

3. From your personal experience as a teen and your observations as a parent, what are some ways peers undermine—intentionally or unintentionally—the authority of parents?

Bad Company, Good Company

In our opening session we discussed the need to form convictions based on God's Word. Remember that having a conviction is "being so thoroughly convinced that something is absolutely true that you take a stand for it regardless of the consequences."

4. Read the following Bible passages:

- Psalm 1:1–3
- Proverbs 13:20
- 1 Corinthians 15:33

What guidance do you find in these verses that can help you form or solidify a biblical conviction about peer pressure?

5. Read Ecclesiastes 4:9–12 and Hebrews 10:24. In what ways can peer pressure be good for your teen?

 HomeBuilders Principle: The friends your teenagers choose play a critical role in the type of people they become.

Your Involvement

6. How does the role of parents in helping a child choose friends often change as the child enters and proceeds through adolescence?

7. Explain why you agree or disagree with the following statement: It's important for adolescent children to have the freedom to choose their own friends with no input or interference from their parents.

Relating to Your Teenagers

8. In what ways can a strong relationship with your child influence how he or she responds to negative peer pressure? If you can, give an example.

9. What ideas have you considered or actually tried in an effort to help your child find the right friends?

 HomeBuilders Principle: The best defense against negative peer pressure is a love-filled relationship between you and your child.

Parent to Parent

It's important for children to learn how to make choices based on biblical convictions rather than what other people pressure them to do. If your child learns to stand strong against negative peer pressure, he or she will have a much greater chance of avoiding the other traps of adolescence.

Consider the following advice:

1. Never underestimate the power of peer pressure on your children.
2. Never assume that the Christian friends of your children are all good influences.

3. Never assume that other Christian families have the same standards you do.
4. Never assume that a friend who has been "good" through elementary school and junior high or middle school will continue to stay that way.
5. Never assume that your ability to discern the truth is greater than your child's ability to deceive you.

At times you'll be tempted to think you're being too harsh by insisting on being involved in helping your child find good friends. Don't back off! Your child's ability to stand against negative peer pressure will be used by God to embed convictions, courage, and a stand-alone faith that will help him or her become a difference maker for good in our culture.

make a date

Set a time for you and your spouse to complete the HomeBuilders project together before the next group meeting. You will be asked at the next session to share an insight or experience from the project.

date _____ time _____

location _____

homebuilders project

On Your Own

1. What was the main impression you came away with from the group meeting?

2. How would you say you handle peer pressure now, as an adult? How would you say your spouse generally handles peer pressure?

3. What are some examples of positive and negative peer pressure in your life?

4. How have you seen your child respond to peer pressure up until now? Be specific.

5. Who are your child's best friends? Make a list.

6. How would you evaluate the friends your child has right now? Which friends are a good influence and which are not? Why?

7. What action steps do you want to apply to your life and parenting approach to guard against the trap of peer pressure?

With Your Spouse

1. Share your responses to the questions you answered on your own.

2. If you identified any problems or potential problems with your child's peer relationships, discuss what you can or should do. If you're comfortable with your child's current peer relationships, discuss what you can do to help support and encourage your child in continuing to make good relationship choices.

3. Discuss the convictions you would like your child to have regarding friends and peer pressure. Review the sample convictions that follow, and then start your own list.

   - Conviction 1: The friends I choose will have a big influence on the kind of person I become.
   - Conviction 2: I will not assume that Christian friends will always be a good influence on me.
   - Conviction 3: To help me stand strong against peer pressure, I will try to decide in advance how I'll respond to key life choices, such as drug and alcohol use or sexual temptations.

4. Close in prayer, with each of you completing the following statement: *"Dear God, my specific prayer for our child and his or her friends is . . ."*

Be sure to check out the related Parent-Teen Interactions beginning on page 79.

3

Sex

You can help your teenagers avoid the trap of sex by challenging them to a high standard of purity and innocence.

warm-up

Sensual Saturation

For this exercise you'll need a variety of magazines—current or old. These could be weeklies, such as *People* or *Time*, but if possible find magazines that are geared primarily toward men, women, or teenagers. Depending on how many magazines you have, break into subgroups of two to four people, with each group assigned a different magazine or two. In your group, go through your magazine(s) looking for examples of advertisements, articles, or photos your group feels are inappropriately sexually suggestive. After each group reports its findings, discuss these questions:

- Were you surprised by what you found? Explain.
- What philosophy do you think lies behind many of these messages?
- How do you think children, especially teenagers, are affected by these types of messages?

Project Report

Share one thing you learned from the HomeBuilders project from the previous session.

Beyond the Birds and the Bees

1. Would you want your children to learn about sex the same way you did? Why or why not?

Case Study

It wasn't hard for Richard to notice that his fourteen-year-old son, Brandon, had developed an interest in the opposite sex. Brandon kept up lively chats on the Internet and texted with different girls from his school.

Richard had told Brandon about "the birds and the bees" several years earlier. But now he wanted to talk with Brandon about much more—the temptations that he was facing as a young teenage boy and the choices he would face about sex and dating. It was just so hard to build up the courage to broach the subject. *He probably wouldn't listen to me anyway*, Richard thought. *Just like I never listened to my parents when it came to sex.*

Of course, now Richard realizes he should have followed his parents' advice. His first sexual experience came at age seventeen, and he had slept with a number of other women over the next few years. But his life changed when he became a Christian during his senior year of college, and he had remained faithful to Brandon's mother. Yet he still felt a lot of guilt about his lifestyle during those years before he came to Christ.

Now, as he thought about speaking to his son, Richard felt like a hypocrite. How could he challenge Brandon to standards he had never come close to meeting when he was a teenager?

2. Many parents today face issues similar to those Richard confronted as they deal with the choices they made in the past. What advice would you give to Richard?

3. What are the potential consequences if children aren't properly taught or guided about sex (or if teens disregard the instruction they've received)?

 HomeBuilders Principle: As a parent, you must take responsibility to teach and model biblical morality and purity.

What Does God's Word Say About Sex?

In a world of shifting standards regarding sexual relations, we need to base our convictions on the truth found in the Bible.

4. With each couple selecting one or more of the following Scripture passages, read your verses with your spouse and discuss the insights these verses offer regarding sex. Then share your verses with the group and report on your insights.

- Genesis 1:27–28
- Genesis 2:22–25
- Proverbs 5:18–19
- Song of Solomon 2:2–7
- 1 Corinthians 7:2–4
- Hebrews 13:4

5. Why do you think God reserves sex for a man and woman to enjoy in the context of marriage? List as many reasons as you can.

Where Do You Draw the Line?

6. If you were to ask the parents in your community what they are teaching their children about sex and morality, what do you think the most common answers would be?

7. On a television news report about churches that are teaching abstinence to their teens, one teenage girl said she would remain a virgin until she was married. But in the

next breath she said that heavy kissing and petting were okay as long as she didn't engage in sexual intercourse. What do you think of this view?

8. What do the following passages tell us about God's standard for sexual purity?

- Romans 16:19

- 1 Corinthians 6:18

- Ephesians 5:3

- 1 Thessalonians 4:3–5

9. What are a few practical things you can do to protect the innocence of your children in today's sex-obsessed culture?

 HomeBuilders Principle: God calls you to protect not only the virginity of your children but also their purity and innocence.

Parent to Parent

When parents make mistakes in teaching their children about sex, it's usually because they assume that their children's convictions and standards are more firmly in place than they really are.

Even if you've done a great job of instructing your children about the biological facts of sex, you need to finish the process with moral training. Of all the discussions we've had in our family about sex, probably 95 percent of them have involved character issues.

Remember:

1. Don't let your own mistakes in this area prevent you from fulfilling your responsibility as a parent.
2. If you don't teach your children about sex and about biblical morality, the world will.
3. It's better to challenge your children to a high standard (with grace) than to no standard at all.
4. Just because a child has made good choices in this area in the past doesn't guarantee that he or she will continue to take a strong stand. The pressure is relentless.

This constant pressure is why your ongoing involvement in your teen's life is so important. You need to develop the type of relationship in which your child feels free to talk with you about these sensitive subjects. And your child needs to know that if he or she fails, you'll show plenty of love and grace even if you're disappointed with the choice made.

make a date

Set a time for you and your spouse to complete the HomeBuilders project together before the next group meeting. You will be asked at the next session to share an insight or experience from the project.

date _____ time _____

location _____

homebuilders project

On Your Own

1. If you're dealing with guilt concerning past sexual sin, this would be a good time to seek forgiveness and cleansing from God. (If you're uncertain how to handle this issue, or how much to divulge to your spouse, we suggest seeking Christian counsel from a spiritually mature individual, pastor, or counselor.) Here are three steps we encourage you to take:

    1. Read Psalm 103:11–14, which speaks of God's forgiveness of our sins.
    2. Pray, confessing your sin to God.
    3. Read 1 John 1:9 as a way to claim with assurance that you've been forgiven.

    If you have questions or doubts about whether you have a personal relationship with God, read the article "Our Problems, God's Answers" on page 97.

2. What did this session reveal to you—good or bad—about how you're doing in giving your teenager guidance for avoiding the trap of sex?

3. What are the biggest concerns you have about the sexual influences on your child?

4. What would you say is the purpose of sex?

Questions 4-7 are designed to help you solidify or formulate your convictions about the trap of premarital sex.

5. How would you reply if your preteen or teenager asked you, "Why is it wrong to have sex before marriage?"

6. How would you rate yourself on how your personal example—your media and entertainment choices, as well as the way you treat your spouse and others of the opposite sex—communicates the principle of sexual purity to your teen?

7. Many parents don't get specific with their teenagers about how far they should go with the opposite sex before marriage. Review the following list. Where do you think your child should draw the line, and why?

- Holding hands
- Being alone with a boyfriend or girlfriend
- Hugging
- Kissing
- French-kissing
- Kissing while lying down
- Touching private areas
- Sexual stimulation
- Sexual intercourse

With Your Spouse

1. Talk through your responses to the questions you answered on your own.

2. Discuss what standards you want to set for your preteen or teen as he or she relates to the opposite sex. Review the sample convictions, and then start your own list.

   - Conviction 1: I will believe and trust in God's view of sex.
   - Conviction 2: I will maintain my purity and innocence until I'm married.

3. Consider what aspects of sex you need to communicate to your child. Talk about when and where these issues should be addressed, and by whom.

4. Pray, asking God to give you wisdom, discernment, and courage as you seek to communicate with and educate your child about sex.

Be sure to check out the related Parent-Teen Interactions beginning on page 79.

4

Dating

One of your greatest challenges as a parent is to set solid dating standards for your teen.

What Would You Do?

It's one thing to talk about setting standards; it's quite another to implement and enforce them. Let's get practical by looking at some real-life situations. With your spouse, select one of the following scenarios to discuss; then report your response to the group.

- Scenario 1: Your daughter, who just turned fourteen, is asked by a seventeen-year-old boy to go to a movie. What would you do?
- Scenario 2: Your fifteen-year-old son has a girlfriend the same age. They want to spend all their time together.

They talk for at least an hour on the phone each night, and she visits often at your home. You become concerned that they're becoming too emotionally attached. What would you do?

- Scenario 3: Your sixteen-year-old son starts dating a girl he met at school. You don't know her or her family, and from the description you've heard from other parents, you wonder if she is a good influence. What would you do?
- Scenario 4: You return home with your spouse late one night and see your seventeen-year-old daughter locked in a passionate embrace with her boyfriend in his car. What would you do? (Would your response be the same if it were your son with his girlfriend?)

Project Report

Share one thing you learned from the HomeBuilders project from the previous session.

Cultural Context

As you may have discovered during the Warm-Up exercise, part of the challenge of discussing "dating" is that the term means different things to different people, and even to different generations. For example, let's say your daughter receives a phone call from a boy she knows from school, and he asks her to go to the school's winter dance. The night of the dance, he picks her up at your home, takes her to the dance, and then drives her home. You might call this a "date," but your daughter may insist that it isn't. Many young people only use the term *dating* when referring to a more serious relationship.

For the benefit of our discussion, keep the following two points in mind: (1) every culture develops some type of system that enables young people to learn how to relate to the opposite sex and find someone to marry, and (2) it's likely that most, if not all, of your children will eventually get married.

As parents, we should evaluate our culture's system (what we generally call "dating") and determine how well it works with our own goals for teaching and training our children about relating to the opposite sex.

1. What are some of the pros and cons regarding how young people today spend time and form relationships with the opposite sex?

2. What positive or negative portrayals of dating relationships do you find in movies and on TV?

3. An issue confronting parents in their children's adolescent years is boyfriend-girlfriend relationships. What are some of the drawbacks of this type of attachment?

Your Responsibility

4. What are the key character qualities or convictions you want your child to have as he or she begins to spend time with friends of the opposite sex?

Answer questions 4 and 5 with your spouse. After answering, you may want to share an appropriate insight or discovery with the group.

5. What training does your child need to become a good spouse?

6. Review the following list of some ways parents can get involved in their teenagers' lives as they begin to date:

- Require your children to show responsibility in different areas (such as completing household chores and keeping up with homework) before being allowed to date.
- Volunteer to be a chaperone for dances and other school functions.
- Encourage your children to use your home as a place to gather with their friends.
- Make an effort to meet and get to know your children's friends of the opposite sex.
- Make an effort to meet the parents of those friends.
- Interview those who go on dates with your children to challenge them to high standards.
- Ask your children on a regular basis how they're doing living up to the standards they've committed to.

Which of these ideas have you tried, and with what result? List other ideas.

HomeBuilders Principle: Your teenagers need your training, guidance, and ongoing involvement as they approach the issue of dating.

Setting Standards

There are a number of issues for you to consider as you set dating standards for your teenagers. These include:

- Character qualities they should display to earn the right to date
- Whether they should have boyfriend-girlfriend relationships
- Dealing with sexual temptation
- When to allow them to begin engaging in activities with the opposite sex—in groups and on a one-on-one date
- Whom they should date
- How they should honor parents—their own and those of the people they date

7. What, if any, standards did your parents have for you when you began to date? What impact did these standards, or lack thereof, have on your dating behavior?

Let's look closer at two of the key issues surrounding dating.

Whom Your Teen Should Date

8. Read 2 Corinthians 6:14–15. How would you apply this passage to your teen's dating relationships?

Dealing with Temptation

9. Read 2 Timothy 2:22. In light of this verse, how would you complete the following sentence: "Pursuing righteousness in dating relationships means that my teen should . . ."

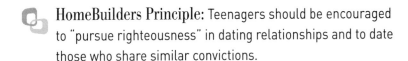 **HomeBuilders Principle:** Teenagers should be encouraged to "pursue righteousness" in dating relationships and to date those who share similar convictions.

Parent to Parent

For us, dating or courting is a small part of the overall process of determining God's will for discovering our life partner in marriage. In our family, the focus hasn't been on dating as much as it's been on training our teens to develop their character as well as their relationships with the opposite sex.

In forming our own convictions as parents about dating, it's not good enough for us just to back off a step or two from what the world says is acceptable. Too many teenagers are being permanently scarred by the dating game. We want to challenge you to develop a fresh approach, prayerfully determine your limits, and train your child to hold fast to them.

A few tips:

1. When setting boundaries for your children, don't underestimate the power of the sex drive.
2. Don't assume a Christian child will be able to make wise choices about whom to date.
3. Don't listen to the culture when it tells you to stay out of the dating lives of your children.

This is a great opportunity for you to train your children in so many important areas—relating to the opposite sex, choosing a spouse, dealing with temptation, and more. Don't let it pass you by . . . get involved!

make a date

Set a time for you and your spouse to complete the HomeBuilders project together before the next group meeting. You will be asked at the next session to share an insight or experience from the project.

date _____ time _____

location _____

homebuilders project

On Your Own

1. What are the main points about dating that seem most relevant to your family situation?

2. What standards did your spouse or in-laws have that you appreciated when you were dating?

3. What aspects of dating do you feel you handled well when dating your spouse?

4. What dating mistakes would you like to see your children avoid?

5. If your child marries, what qualities would you want to be most evident in your son's or daughter's future spouse?

6. What one thing could you do in a more intentional way to train or model for your teen how to be an excellent spouse?

Family Dating Guidelines

7. What do you think would be some reasonable standards to set for your teenagers in each of the following areas? Write down one standard under each item listed.

- Character qualities they should display to earn the right to date

- Whether they should have boyfriend-girlfriend relationships

- How to deal with sexual temptation

- When to allow them to begin engaging in activities with the opposite sex—in groups and on a one-on-one date

- Whom they should date

- How they should honor parents—their own and those of the people they date

With Your Spouse

1. Share your responses to the questions you answered on your own.

2. Tell each other what you wrote down as "Family Dating Guidelines" under question 7 in the previous section. Discuss the benefits of having a formal list of dating guidelines. If you were to adopt a list of guidelines, what items do you agree need to be included?

3. Discuss the convictions about dating you would like to see your teen form. Review the following sample convictions, and then write your own.

   - Conviction 1: Until I'm much older, I will concentrate on building friendships, not romantic emotional attachments, with the opposite sex.
   - Conviction 2: I need to accept my parents' involvement and heed their judgment when it comes to issues surrounding time spent with the opposite sex.
   - Conviction 3: I need to treat members of the opposite sex wisely and honorably.

4. Close in prayer. Pray specifically for each of your children and for the relationships in their lives.

Be sure to check out the related Parent-Teen Interactions beginning on page 79.

5

Media

Teenagers need to develop discernment about the type and amount of media they consume.

Media Log

Thinking back to yesterday, how much time did you spend reading, watching, or listening to various kinds of entertainment or news-based media? Take a minute to fill out the following log, based on your best estimates, and then discuss the questions that follow.

Type	Time
Music/Radio	
TV/Movies	
Internet	
Newspapers/Magazines	

Type	Time
Books	
Video Games	
Social Networking	
Other:	
TOTAL:	

- What was your total?
- How do you think the amount of media you consumed yesterday would compare with that of your teen?
- What do you see as good or bad about the variety of media you use on any given day?

Project Report

Share one thing you learned from the HomeBuilders project from the previous session.

Media Saturation

Every day we're bombarded with messages from media sources and offered an array of choices, all competing for our time and attention. We need to take time to evaluate how this flood of media affects us—and our children.

There are two areas we need to focus on as we evaluate the impact of media on our lives:

- the time we devote to media
- the content of the media

1. Why do you think media can be such a trap for teenagers? In what ways have you seen your teen affected by the content of the media he or she chooses to watch, read, or listen to?

2. How do you think it would affect your family if you took a drastic step to limit the use of media in your home? For example, what would happen if you . . .

   - abolished television (including movies) for a week? a month? for good?

   - limited the recreational use of the Internet (Web surfing, social media, video watching, etc.) to one hour per week of "screen time" per person?

3. In what ways can too much exposure to media hurt your relationship with your children—especially teenagers?

HomeBuilders Principle: Media must not replace relationships or relationship building in a family.

Worthless Things

Psalm 101:2–4 states, "I will ponder the way that is blameless. Oh when will you come to me? I will walk with integrity of heart within my house; I will not set before my eyes anything that is worthless. I hate the work of those who fall away; it shall not cling to me."

4. What, in your opinion, are examples from media of worthless things that should be avoided?

5. Read Colossians 2:8. How can the "philosophy and empty deceit" presented in the media undermine your faith and take you and your children captive?

6. Read Ephesians 4:17–19. How can the media we expose ourselves to gradually harden our hearts toward God and dull our sensitivities?

HomeBuilders Principle: Your media choices will affect your relationship with God.

Setting Standards

With such a bewildering array of media choices confronting us, and with so much filth just a click away, many parents are unprepared to handle the onslaught of media upon their families. More than ever it's critical for us to set solid standards for ourselves and our children.

7. Why do you think parents—both Christians and non-Christians—have such varying standards about media? Do you think parents are generally too strict or too lenient when it comes to the boundaries they set?

8. Read Philippians 4:8. On a practical level, how would you relate this passage to the issue of setting media standards for you and your children?

9. How good are you at keeping track of your teen's media interests and choices? How could you do a better job?

Answer question 9 with your spouse. After answering, you may want to share an appropriate insight or discovery with the group.

 HomeBuilders Principle: You must take responsibility to screen the media used by your family and to set limits.

Parent to Parent

Too many parents allow media to overwhelm their families because they haven't thought through a plan for passing on clear convictions to their children. They haven't taken a good look at their own convictions, and often they haven't talked about guidelines for what their children should watch, read, and listen to.

One thing is certain: The media is becoming more and more pervasive. It can eat up our time, corrupt our morals, and erode our trust in the truth of God's Word. We encourage you to work carefully through this week's HomeBuilders project and begin setting some clear convictions and guidelines.

Some truths to remember:

1. Never underestimate the influence of the media in your life or the lives of your children.
2. Never underestimate the ability of your children to hide what they're doing.
3. Don't assume that your children won't be lured to an Internet chat room, message board, or Web site that contains immoral or dangerous content.
4. Your children's "right to privacy" doesn't override your responsibilities as a parent. Don't be afraid to be a snoop! Find out what media choices your children are making. Ask questions, look through their rooms, and install special software on your computer to monitor Web activity—do whatever it takes!

make a date

Set a time for you and your spouse to complete the HomeBuilders project together before the next group meeting. You will be asked at the next session to share an insight or experience from the project.

date _____ time _____

location _____

homebuilders project

On Your Own

1. What insight or concepts from this session do you most need to apply?

2. Revisit the Warm-Up exercise. Calculate how much time you spent yesterday consuming various forms of media. If you can, make the same calculation for your teen(s).

3. How would you evaluate the amount of time you and your children spent with media today (note below with an S for yourself and initials for each of your teens)?

   ___ Way too much time
   ___ Too much time
   ___ Just about the right amount of time
   ___ Not enough time
   ___ Other: _____

4. What media-use patterns are you observing in your teen(s) that concern you?

5. In what ways do you think your own media habits affect your children?

6. What could you or your teen(s) do—or do better—if you reduced the amount of time you spent on media?

7. Concerning your personal tastes in media, are you regularly watching, listening to, or reading material that you would be embarrassed to watch, read, or listen to with your preteen or teen?

8. Read Titus 2:11–12. On what basis can you say no to things that aren't good for you? What changes do you need to make in the media standards you have for yourself? for your children?

With Your Spouse

1. Share your responses to the questions you answered on your own.

2. Based on what you've learned in this session, as well as your understanding of Scripture, discuss the convictions you want to claim in the area of media. Review the sample convictions, and then write your own.

   - Conviction 1: I need to allow Jesus Christ to be Lord over all forms of media that I allow in my life.
   - Conviction 2: I need to learn how to discern between good and evil in the media, because what I allow to come into my mind can affect the way I think and live.
   - Conviction 3: I need to stand firm and turn away from media temptations quickly.

3. Talk about specific guidelines you would like to have for your family in the media categories that follow, and how you can begin communicating them to your children.

   - TV/movies
   - Internet
   - social networking
   - video games
   - music/radio
   - cell phones/texting

- books/magazines
- Other: _____

4. Pray about the standards you should have in the area of media. Ask God to give you wisdom in setting, modeling, and enforcing appropriate media standards.

COMING ATTRACTIONS

Here's something you can do to help yourself and your children make informed choices about the movies and DVDs you watch. (Do this as a couple or as a family.)

Visit an Internet site that evaluates movies (such as ScreenIt.com, PluggedIn.com, or MinistryandMedia.com). Look up a movie that you or your children want to see. Read the reviews, and then discuss these questions:

- How does having this information influence your choice?
- Do you find information like this helpful in making movie-viewing choices? Explain.

Be sure to check out the related Parent-Teen Interactions beginning on page 79.

6

Substance
Abuse

Your connectedness with your teen, your integrity, and your walk with God will help your child deal with one of the deadliest traps of adolescence.

warm-up

Addiction

Choose one of the following questions to answer, and then share your response with the group:

- How common was the use of drugs and alcohol in your high school? How do you think this compares with your teen's school?
- Why do you think some parents find it uncomfortable or threatening to discuss the topic of substance abuse with their kids?

- If you can, tell the group about someone you know who developed a problem with alcohol or drugs. How did this person first start using these substances? How did the problem affect his or her life and family?

Project Report

Share one thing you learned from the HomeBuilders project from the previous session.

blueprints

Few families are untouched by the trap of substance abuse. Many people can name at least one relative who has a problem with alcohol, drugs, or painkillers. Add substances like cigarettes, inhalants, and diet pills, and you'll find even more people struggling with some form of addiction—including many who don't know they're addicted.

One of the greatest fears for parents is that somehow their child will be caught in this trap.

Temptation

1. What do you think are the primary reasons so many teenagers choose to experiment with alcohol, tobacco, or drugs?

2. As a group, see how many reasons you can list for why children should avoid these types of substances. Then read 1 Corinthians 6:19–20. What additional insight(s) do you find in this passage?

3. What type of home environment do you feel would give your children the best protection against falling into the trap of substance abuse?

Connectedness

When dealing with this life-and-death issue, it's vitally important for parents to stay connected with their teenage children by knowing what's going on in their lives. Often parents don't know as much about their kids as they think they do. In one survey, for example, both parents and teens were asked what percentage of their child's life the parents knew about. The parents' answers ranged from 60 to 80 percent, while most of the children said 25 to 50 percent.

4. What do you think of the following actions parents could take to find out if their teenagers are sampling abusive substances? Rate each action on the agree-disagree scale, and then explain your answers to the group.

Asking your teens if they're smoking, drinking, or taking drugs

1	2	3	4
Strongly Agree	Somewhat Agree	Somewhat Disagree	Strongly Disagree

Waiting up for teens to return home and smelling their breath before they go to bed

1	2	3	4
Strongly Agree	Somewhat Agree	Somewhat Disagree	Strongly Disagree

Searching your teen's room, clothes, or automobile

1	2	3	4
Strongly Agree	Somewhat Agree	Somewhat Disagree	Strongly Disagree

Calling a parent whose teen is hosting a party and asking if alcohol or drugs will be present

1	2	3	4
Strongly Agree	Somewhat Agree	Somewhat Disagree	Strongly Disagree

Showing up uninvited at a teen party

1	2	3	4
Strongly Agree	Somewhat Agree	Somewhat Disagree	Strongly Disagree

Asking other teenagers what they know about substance abuse in your teen's school

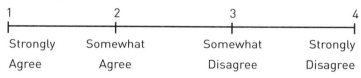

1	2	3	4
Strongly Agree	Somewhat Agree	Somewhat Disagree	Strongly Disagree

 HomeBuilders Principle: To help your teenagers avoid abusive substances, you must stay connected by knowing what is happening in their lives and by giving them plenty of attention, discipline, guidance, acceptance, and love.

Modeling Integrity

Throughout this study we've talked about your role as a model—a living picture of how to make choices with integrity. Psalm 101:2 tells us, "I will ponder the way that is blameless. . . . I will walk with integrity of heart within my house."

5. Why is the example you set particularly important in the area of substance abuse?

6. What are your personal standards regarding substance abuse? From the following list, pick one or two items and tell the group about your personal standards for each.

- alcohol
- cigarettes
- chewing tobacco
- marijuana
- inhalants (adhesives, aerosols, solvents, and gases)
- illicit drugs (such as cocaine and Ecstasy)
- over-the-counter drugs (such as diet pills)
- prescription drugs (such as painkillers)
- Other: _____

 HomeBuilders Principle: Your example of high personal standards regarding harmful substances will help minimize your child's opportunity to have any excuse to abuse alcohol or drugs.

Modeling a Walk with God

For many people, substance abuse begins with an attempt to escape from reality or search for fulfillment in life from things and people that are often harmful. But real life is found in a relationship with God. King David testified to this in Psalm 16:11, praising God and declaring, "You make known to me the path of life; in your presence there is fullness of joy; at your right hand are pleasures forevermore."

7. If you're comfortable sharing, briefly tell the group how you came to be a Christ follower, and how this relationship has changed your life.

8. Why is it critical for your teens to have a personal relationship with God as they negotiate not only the trap of substance abuse but all the various traps of adolescence?

9. Read Psalm 78:5–8. How can you apply this passage to help ensure that your child will remain faithful to God? What can you do to model your trust in God to your children?

HomeBuilders Principle: Teaching and modeling a rich love relationship with Jesus Christ as a parent will help your children develop their own trust in God and learn how to translate the wisdom they find in Scripture into their lives and choices.

Reflections

As you come to the end of this course, take a few minutes to reflect on the experience. Review the following questions and write down responses to the questions you can answer. Then share with the group one or more of your responses.

- What has this group meant to you over the course of this study? Be specific.

- What is the most valuable principle you've learned or discovered?

- How have you as a parent been changed or challenged through this study?

- What would you like to see happen next for this group?

One of the great benefits of completing this HomeBuilders study with other parents is that you've been able to encourage one another to be consistently involved with your children as they move through adolescence. We challenge you to continue this involvement by doing three things:

- Pray regularly for one another and for your children.
- Keep in touch. Contact one another for advice and encouragement as you face different issues with your children.
- Keep in touch with one another's children.

Other people can see qualities in your children—both good and bad—that you may not. Make a special effort to tell your friends about good things you've seen their children do. But also give your friends permission to pass on any concerns they may have about your children. This is difficult to do. You'll need to give one another a lot of grace in this area. But if you see a friend's child do something you know isn't right, or if you see that child in a compromising situation, it may be more dangerous not to tell the parent.

Parent to Parent

Though you may not realize it, this entire study has given you an opportunity to apply the words of Psalm 78:5–8 in your family. As you've studied the different traps of adolescence, we've exhorted you to put your confidence in God and the Bible, and to experience the Lord's guidance and leading. Your assignment as a parent is to teach your children to do the same.

Parenting isn't an exact science. You can develop a wonderful relationship with your children, guide them with a good balance of love and discipline, and encourage them to form God-honoring convictions. Eventually your children will grow up, leave your home, and make their own choices. In the end, they need their own faith. They need to learn on their own to put their confidence in God. As a parent, your greatest privilege and responsibility is showing them, on a daily basis, how to trust God in every area of life.

Some tips:

1. When it comes to substance abuse, your child's personal rights don't usurp your parental responsibility to snoop.
2. Don't become predictable with your teenager. Find fresh and surprising ways to ensure that they're staying away from abusive substances.
3. Don't assume that other parents share your standards regarding alcohol and drugs.
4. What you do in moderation, your children will be tempted to do in excess.
5. Nobody raises perfect children. In the end, they'll make their own choices in life.
6. Our hope as parents is in God and his faithfulness.

make a date

Set a time for you and your spouse to complete the HomeBuilders project together.

date _____ time _____

location _____

homebuilders project

On Your Own

1. Congratulations—you've made it to the last project of this study! Reflect on what impact this course has had on you by answering these questions:

   • What has been the best part of this study for you?

   • How has this study benefited your marriage?

   • In what ways has this study helped you as a parent?

   • What new thing have you learned or discovered about your spouse? about yourself? about your teen?

2. What was the most important insight or lesson for you from this session?

3. Did your parents drink, smoke, or use drugs? What impact has the example of your parents had on you?

4. What, if any, substances that you regularly use might give your teen the impression that you need those substances to be happy or to deal with life?

5. How comfortable would you be if your children were to adopt the same standards you have for the various substances that were discussed in this session? Why?

6. Do you have a teen who you think may have tried or is likely to try alcohol, cigarettes, or drugs? Explain.

7. How would you assess the spiritual life of your children? What do they need to develop or deepen in their relationship with God? (For more information on a personal relationship with God, read the article "Our Problems, God's Answers" starting on page 97.)

8. Thinking about this course overall, what is at least one point of action you've identified as something you want to do, stop doing, or change? What do you need to do to turn this action point into a reality?

With Your Spouse

1. Discuss your responses to the questions you answered on your own.

2. Review the following sample convictions regarding substance abuse, and then work on starting your own list. Talk through the convictions you would like your children to have and how best to communicate these standards.

   - Conviction 1: I will honor and protect my own body because it "is a temple of the Holy Spirit" (1 Corinthians 6:19).
   - Conviction 2: I will decide in advance what I'll do when presented with the opportunity to smoke, drink alcohol, or use other substances.

3. Evaluate what you can do to continue to strengthen your home. You may want to consider continuing the practice of setting aside time for date nights. You may also want to look at the list of ideas on page 95.

4. Close in prayer, thanking God for one another and for your children. Pray for God's wisdom and direction as you continue to seek to guide your teenagers.

Be sure to check out the related Parent-Teen Interactions beginning on page 79.

parent-teen interactions

Interaction 1

The Traps of Adolescence

1. Take your teen or preteen out for a casual dinner or dessert. After you've talked awhile, tell your teen about the HomeBuilders group you're a part of. Describe the purpose of the study, which is to talk about how to help teenagers deal with the "traps of adolescence"—the key issues all teens face (including you when you were that age), such as peer pressure, sex, dating, media, and alcohol and drugs. Explain that part of the study involves a series of short projects for parents to complete with their teenagers (or preteens).

2. Tell your teenager: For the next few minutes, think of me as a television or newspaper reporter conducting an interview with you to get your opinion on the key issues teenagers face.

3. Ask your teen the questions that follow. Avoid the temptation to talk, except to ask follow-up or clarifying questions. Encourage your teen to reply honestly, but let him or her know it's okay to pass on a question. The purpose of this first interaction is simply for you to listen to your son or daughter. This is your time to listen, not talk.

- What would you say is the biggest problem teenagers face today?
- What does it take to be part of the "in" crowd at your school?
- When it comes to the subject of sex, is abstinence respected or made fun of? Explain.
- To you, what qualifies as a "date"? Give an example of what a date is and isn't.
- Which musical artists or groups and radio stations are popular with the kids in your class?
- Would you say that the use of drugs at your school is greater than adults think, or less? What about alcohol use? Explain.
- Is there anything you would like to tell me about the issues teens face that I haven't asked?

Interaction 2

Peer Pressure

Use the following exercise to drive home a memorable lesson to your teen about how the friends we hang out with can have a big influence on our lives.

This interaction is based on the saying "One bad apple can spoil the whole barrel." Though this phrase no longer carries much meaning in a day when most of us buy apples by the bag and store them only for a short time, your teen won't forget seeing what happens when you put a bad apple in with some good ones.

You'll need three or four apples for this interaction. One of the apples needs to be damaged or bruised badly. (You can use other kinds of produce if you like. Tomatoes, lettuce, or an orange will work quickly.

1. Show the apples or produce to your teen and explain that the good apples represent teenagers who are making good choices when dealing with such issues as smoking, drinking, talking profanely, and being obedient to their parents. Then ask: With that in mind, what do you think the bruised apple represents?

2. Tell your teenager that this illustration will show what happens when good apples spend too much time with bad apples. Put the apples together in a plastic bag— preferably a self-sealing one, and with your teen find a warm, dark place to put the bag. Explain that you'll come back to see what happened at a later time (perhaps in a few weeks or months, depending on how long you want this experiment to run).

3. Now have your teenager read 1 Corinthians 15:33 aloud. Ask: What do you think this verse means? How does "bad company" corrupt us?

4. Ask: What does this verse say to you about the type of friends you should choose?

5. Talk with your teenager about the apples—other teens— in his or her life. Ask: Which of your friends influence you to do what's right?

6. Together, read Psalm 1:1–3. Ask: What do you think it means to walk in the "counsel of the wicked," stand in the "way of sinners," or sit in the "seat of scoffers"?

7. Then ask: Who do you know that isn't the best influence on you?

8. Be sure to note that it's impossible to live in our world without having friends who aren't the best of influences. In fact, God calls us to be good influences on those "bad apples" by showing them the love of Christ. It's important, however, to make sure you aren't allowing those bad influences to lead you into making poor choices.

9. Close your time in prayer, asking God to give your teen the ability to discern the good apples and the bruised apples among his or her friends.

At a Later Date

1. Check the apples to make sure they've all turned into a brownish, putrid mush. Then take your teenager with you to retrieve the apples from where you stored them. Ask: How is this like what happens to us when we spend time with friends who are bad influences?

2. Read 1 Corinthians 15:33 again, and ask your teen: Since we first talked about this subject, what additional things have you noticed about your friends? Who are the good influences, and who aren't as good?

Interaction 3

Sex

This interaction is divided into two sections. Part 1 is titled "What Does God Say About Sex?" It leads you through scriptures and questions that give you the opportunity to talk with your teen about biblical standards on sexual purity. Part 2, "Where Do You Draw the Line?" provides an object lesson on how easy it is for your teen to lose his or her innocence and then challenges your teen to verbalize his or her convictions. By doing this, you call your teen to accountability and create a future opportunity to talk further about this subject. You're encouraged to do both parts. Depending on your schedule, you may want to complete each of them on separate occasions.

Part 1: What Does God Say About Sex?

Note: Because this subject can be challenging to discuss with your teen, for the questions that follow, you may want to refer to your notes from the corresponding questions (4, 5, and 8) in session 3 (pages 30-33). There are also related commentary notes for these questions (numbered as 4, 5, and 8) on pages 123-125.

1. Have your teen read each of the following scriptures. After each one, ask: What does this passage tell us about sex?

   - Genesis 1:27–28
   - Genesis 2:22–25
   - Proverbs 5:18–19
   - 1 Corinthians 7:2–4
   - Hebrews 13:4

2. Ask: Why do you think God reserves sex for a man and woman to enjoy in the context of marriage?

3. Now have your teen read 1 Corinthians 6:18 and 1 Thessalonians 4:3–5. Ask: What do these verses tell us about

God's standards for sexual purity? What do you think it means to "flee from sexual immorality" and "abstain from sexual immorality"?

4. Read Romans 16:19. Ask: What do you think it means to be "innocent as to what is evil"? How would you apply this to the subject of sexual morality?

Part 2: Where Do You Draw the Line?

For the following exercise, you need a needle and two balloons filled with water. Be sure to experiment beforehand to ensure you get the proper effect.

The first balloon should be small, so that when it's filled as full as you can get it while still being able to tie it off, it will burst when stuck with a pin. This demonstration will be used to illustrate how you can lose all your purity and innocence at once.

The second balloon should be strong and large enough so that when you fill it with water and actually prick it with a needle, it won't burst but will dribble out a drop or two, and if you squeeze it, it will shoot out a stream of water. Both the droplets and stream illustrate how sexual involvement can progress in a teenager's life, with purity and innocence being lost gradually and imperceptibly at first, and then the cumulative effect of little choices becomes a steady stream that drains away any purity that remains.

1. Pick up the smaller water balloon first. Say: This water balloon is filled with your sexual purity and innocence. This is all that you have. How much of it would you want to give away before you're married?

2. Then say: Let's say in a couple of years you meet the boy or girl of your dreams. The physical attraction is too strong, and you decide that just this once you're going to sleep with him or her. What happens to your purity? (With your needle, tear a large hole in the smaller water balloon so that all the water gushes out.)

3. Now pick up the larger water balloon. Then say: That's one way to lose all of your purity and innocence. Now let's say that you date someone who just wants a little kiss, your first kiss and just a little bit of your innocence, and you agree. (Hold the balloon up and pierce it with a needle.) Say: You think to yourself, "What's the big deal? It's just a little drop. I'll never miss it."

4. Continue: Then someone else comes along, and you date for a while, and this person just wants a little droplet. He or she says, "Let's make out in the car." So you give the person a little more of your innocence. (Stick the needle in the balloon again a few more times.)

5. Then let's say you really like someone, and you start to get serious. You decide it's okay to give away even more of your purity and innocence. (Continue sticking the needle in the balloon until the water is all gone.)

6. Say: That relationship ends, and a few years later you finally meet the person you're going to marry. Then ask: So now, as you approach your wedding night, how much of your purity will you have to give to the one you marry and spend the rest of your life with?

7. Say: That's how young people today are losing one of the most precious gifts that they can give to another human

being, and they start by giving their purity and innocence away a drop at a time. Then they give away even more, and as the holes get larger, the drops become a small stream.

8. Finally, ask your teen: Knowing what you now know about losing your purity and innocence, where would you draw the line about how far you're going to go with the opposite sex before marriage?

Interaction 4

Dating

To talk with your teen about dating, we encourage you to take him or her out for a date. Often the father is the one who does this, especially with daughters, but you may want the mother to take out a son, so he'll hear a woman's perspective on this issue. Any combination will work. What's important is that you make the effort to connect with your teen about dating. Don't worry about saying everything perfectly.

1. Set a time to take your teen out, and decide what the setting will be. A nice restaurant that is conducive to conversation without distractions works well. Call or write a note to your teen and make the invitation special. If you've never done this before, you may feel a bit awkward, but don't let this get in the way of meeting this important need in your teen.

   Before your date, give your teen a copy of the Dating Questionnaire (on page 88) to fill out prior to your date.

2. Dress as if you're going on an important date. You're helping your child see and set a standard that will guide his or her social life. Besides, if you dress nicely, it will give the event a feeling of importance. Be sure to bring with you a Bible and this book, or write down on index cards the verses and questions from points 4 and 5.

3. As you begin your time together, simply remind your son or daughter that you need to discuss dating with him or her as part of your study. Tell your teen that you want this date to be an example of how he or she should treat someone else or be treated on a date. Then ask how he or she answered the questions on the Dating Questionnaire.

4. After hearing your teen's answers to the Dating Questionnaire, read the following verses:

   - 2 Corinthians 6:14–15
   - Philippians 4:8
   - 2 Timothy 2:22
     Then discuss these questions:
   - How do you think these verses should be applied to how you relate to the opposite sex?
   - What standards do these verses point you to regarding your social life?

5. Together draft some guidelines that you and your teen agree should be part of his or her social and dating life. Before you begin writing these standards, read Proverbs 1:8–9. Ask your teen: How can teens apply this passage to the subject of dating?

DATING QUESTIONNAIRE

1. What is the purpose of dating?

2. What is a date?

3. How old should you be to date? Why?

4. If you were a parent, when would you let your child begin dating?

5. When should you be able to double-date?

6. Would you choose to date only Christians? Why?

Permission to photocopy this page from HOMEBUILDERS PARENTING SERIES®: Guiding Your Teenagers granted for local church use.

Interaction 5

Media

In this project you'll talk with your teen about the different ways media affect us. You'll also begin to teach him or her how to discern the variety of messages in the media. You'll watch a television show together (or a movie, if you wish) and talk about the various philosophies promoted in the show and its advertisements.

Before doing this interaction, be sure to work through the HomeBuilders project with your spouse and decide on some family standards for media.

1. With your teen, create a list of all the opportunities in your home to consume different types of media. Have your son or daughter write down which types of media devices or sources there are in each room of your home—radios, televisions, DVD players, MP3 or CD players, books, magazines, computers, and video games. You and your teen may want to actually walk through your home as you compile this list.

2. Ask your teen the following questions: In what ways do you think all these types of media affect us? How do they affect our minds? How do they affect our family? How do they affect our walk with God?

3. Have your teen read Psalm 101:2–4 and Philippians 4:8. Then ask: How would you relate these passages to the issue of how we entertain ourselves with media?

4. Ask: What would you say is an example of a worthless or vile thing that your friends have seen or heard recently in the media?

5. Ask: What is an example of something you've seen or heard that's worthless or vile?

6. Watch a television show (or a movie) together. Be sure not to skip the commercials.

7. When you're finished, ask: What were some of the different values this show promoted? How do these values compare to what we know to be true in God's Word?

8. Then ask about the advertisements: What were the ads trying to get us to do? What methods are they utilizing to persuade us? What values are they promoting? How do these values compare to what we know to be true in the Word of God?

9. Share with your teen the guidelines you and your spouse discussed in the "Media" session's HomeBuilders project. Explain why you're setting these standards.

Interaction 6

Substance Abuse

1. For this interaction we suggest taking your teen to a meeting of Alcoholics Anonymous. This type of experience can leave a lasting impression. There are thousands of AA chapters throughout the United States. To find one near you, look up "Alcoholics Anonymous" in the phone book, on the Internet, or talk to someone on staff at your church (or at your place of work). Ideally, find someone who is an AA member and would be willing to serve as your host for a visit to a meeting.

2. After attending the meeting, take your teen out for a treat and ask the following questions:

   - What were your impressions of the meeting?
   - Were you surprised by anything at the meeting?
   - What did you think of what the people there had to say?
   - How do you think their addictions have changed their lives?

3. Read Romans 12:1–2. Ask: What do you think it means to present our bodies to the Lord as a "living sacrifice" that is holy and acceptable to him?

4. Ask: On a practical level, how can we present our bodies to the Lord? When or how often should this take place?

5. Ask: How do you think the concept of being a living sacrifice to the Lord applies to the subject of drugs and alcohol?

6. Conclude this outing by asking your teen to decide in advance what he or she would do in each of the following situations:

   - You're walking home from school, and a friend pulls out a cigarette. He asks you if you want one too. You say no, and he says, "Why don't you just try it? One little cigarette isn't going to hurt you." What do you do, and why?
   - A friend is having a small party with several other girls and boys from your high school. One of the girls brings in a cooler full of beer and starts handing it out. What do you do, and why?

FOR EXTRA IMPACT

1. Plan a time with your teenage children (or you can include the entire family if you want) in which you do something active for at least four hours or more. Go out and play games, take a hike, go to the zoo, clean the yard together, play softball—anything to get good and dirty and sweaty. Whatever you do, make sure you have fun together!

2. Here's the catch: When you're finished, don't take a bath or shower until the next day! Continue with your other activities throughout the rest of the day. Talk about how it feels to be so dirty. Don't be in a hurry. Enjoy this interaction as a family. Make some jokes—have fun with this.

3. The following morning, before showers or baths, prepare a nice breakfast and, while you eat together, ask your family: How has it felt to be so dirty for so long? What was it like trying to sleep last night?

4. Ask: What kinds of things make the inside of our bodies dirty?

5. Discuss: How do these things make our bodies dirty?

where do you go from here?

We hope that you have benefited from this study in the Home-Builders Parenting Series and that your marriage and family will continue to grow as you submit to Jesus Christ and build according to his blueprints. We also hope that you will reach out to strengthen other marriages in your local church and community. Your influence is needed.

A favorite World War II story illustrates this point clearly.

The year was 1940. The French army had just collapsed under Hitler's onslaught. The Dutch had folded, overwhelmed by the Nazi regime. The Belgians had surrendered. And the British army was trapped on the coast of France in the channel port of Dunkirk.

Two hundred twenty thousand of Britain's finest young men seemed doomed to die, turning the English Channel red with their blood. The Fuehrer's troops, only miles away in the hills of France, didn't realize how close to victory they actually were.

Any attempt at rescue seemed futile in the time remaining. A thin British navy—the professionals—told King George VI that they could save 17,000 troops at best. The House of Commons was warned to prepare for "hard and heavy tidings."

Politicians were paralyzed. The king was powerless. And the Allies could only watch as spectators from a distance. Then as the doom of the British army seemed imminent, a strange fleet appeared on the horizon of the English Channel—the wildest assortment of boats perhaps ever assembled in history. Trawlers, tugs, scows, fishing sloops, lifeboats, pleasure craft, smacks and coasters, sailboats, even the London fire-brigade flotilla. Ships manned by civilian volunteers—English fathers joining in the rescue of Britain's exhausted, bleeding sons.

William Manchester writes in his epic novel *The Last Lion* that what happened in 1940 at Dunkirk seems like a miracle. Not only were most of the British soldiers rescued but 118,000 other Allied troops as well.

Today the Christian home is much like those troops at Dunkirk—pressured, trapped, demoralized, and in need of help. The Christian community may be much like England—waiting for professionals to step in and save the family. But the problem is much too large for them to solve alone.

We need an all-out effort by men and women "sailing" to rescue the exhausted and wounded families. We need an outreach effort by common couples with faith in an uncommon God. For too long, married couples within the church have abdicated to those in full-time vocational ministry the privilege and responsibility of influencing others.

We challenge you to invest your lives in others, to join in the rescue. You and other couples around the world can team together to build thousands of marriages and families and, in doing so, continue to strengthen your own.

Be a HomeBuilder

Here are some practical ways you can make a difference in families today:

- Gather a group of four to seven couples and lead them through this HomeBuilders study. Consider challenging others in your church or community to form additional HomeBuilders groups.
- Commit to continue building families and marriages by doing another small-group study in the HomeBuilders Parenting Series or the HomeBuilders Couples Series.
- Consider using the *JESUS* film as an outreach. For more information contact FamilyLife at the number or Web site below.
- Host a dinner party. Invite families from your neighborhood to your home, and as a couple share your faith in Christ.
- If you have attended FamilyLife's Weekend to Remember getaway, consider offering to assist your pastor in counseling engaged couples, using the material you received.

For more information about these ministry opportunities, contact your local church or

FamilyLife
PO Box 7111
Little Rock, AR 72223
1-800-FL-TODAY
FamilyLife.com

our problems, God's answers

Every couple has to deal with problems in marriage—communication problems, money problems, difficulties with sexual intimacy, and more. Learning how to handle these issues is important to cultivating a strong and loving relationship.

The Big Problem

One basic problem is at the heart of every other problem in marriage, and it's too big for any person to deal with on his or her own. The problem is separation from God. If you want to experience life and marriage the way they were designed to be, you need a vital relationship with the God who created you.

But sin separates us from God. Some try to deal with sin by working hard to become better people. They may read books on how to control anger, or they may resolve to stop cheating on their taxes, but in their hearts they know—we all know—that the sin problem runs much deeper than bad habits and will take more than our best behavior to overcome it. In reality, we have rebelled against God. We have ignored him and have decided to run our lives in a way that makes sense to us, thinking that our ideas and plans are better than his.

> For all have sinned and fall short of the glory of God.
> (Romans 3:23)

What does it mean to "fall short of the glory of God"? It means that none of us has trusted and treasured God the way we should. We have sought to satisfy ourselves with other things and have treated them as more valuable than God. We have gone our own way. According to the Bible, we have to pay a penalty for our sin. We cannot simply do things the way we choose and hope it will be okay with God. Following our own plans leads to our destruction.

There is a way that seems right to a man, but its end is
the way to death. (Proverbs 14:12)

For the wages of sin is death. (Romans 6:23)

The penalty for sin is that we are separated from God's love. God is holy, and we are sinful. No matter how hard we try, we cannot come up with some plan, like living a good life or even trying to do what the Bible says, and hope that we can avoid the penalty.

God's Solution to Sin

Thankfully, God has a way to solve our dilemma. He became a man through the person of Jesus Christ. Jesus lived a holy life in perfect obedience to God's plan. He also willingly died on a cross to pay our penalty for sin. Then he proved that he is more powerful than sin or death by rising from the dead. He alone has the power to overrule the penalty for our sin.

Jesus said to him, "I am the way, and the truth, and
the life. No one comes to the Father except through me."
(John 14:6)

But God shows his love for us in that while we were
still sinners, Christ died for us. (Romans 5:8)

For the wages of sin is death, but the free gift of
God is eternal life in Christ Jesus our Lord. (Romans
6:23)

The death and resurrection of Jesus have fixed our sin problem. He has bridged the gap between God and us. He is calling us
to come to him and to give up our flawed plans for running our
lives. He wants us to trust God and his plan.

Accepting God's Solution

If you recognize that you are separated from God, he is calling
you to confess your sins. All of us have made messes of our lives
because we have stubbornly preferred our ideas and plans to his.
As a result, we deserve to be cut off from God's love and his care
for us. But God has promised that if we will acknowledge that we
have rebelled against his plan, he will forgive us and will fix our
sin problem.

But to all who did receive him, who believed in his
name, he gave the right to become children of God.
(John 1:12)

For by grace you have been saved through faith. And
this is not your own doing; it is the gift of God, not a
result of works, so that no one may boast. (Ephesians
2:8–9)

When the Bible talks about receiving Christ, it means we acknowledge that we are sinners and that we can't fix the problem ourselves. It means we turn away from our sin. And it means we trust Christ to forgive our sins and to make us the kind of people he wants us to be. It's not enough to intellectually believe that Christ is the Son of God. We must trust in him and his plan for our lives by faith, as an act of the will.

Are things right between you and God, with him and his plan at the center of your life? Or is life spinning out of control as you seek to make your own way?

If you have been trying to make your own way, you can decide today to change. You can turn to Christ and allow him to transform your life. All you need to do is talk to him and tell him what is stirring in your mind and in your heart. If you've never done this, consider taking the steps listed here:

- Do you agree that you need God? Tell God.
- Have you made a mess of your life by following your own plan? Tell God.
- Do you want God to forgive you? Tell God.
- Do you believe that Jesus' death on the cross and his resurrection from the dead gave him the power to fix your sin problem and to grant you the free gift of eternal life? Tell God.
- Are you ready to acknowledge that God's plan for your life is better than any plan you could come up with? Tell God.
- Do you agree that God has the right to be the Lord and Master of your life? Tell God.

Seek the LORD while he may be found; call upon him while he is near. (Isaiah 55:6)

Here is a suggested prayer:

Lord Jesus, I need you. Thank you for dying on the cross for my sins. I receive you as my Savior and Lord. Thank you for forgiving my sins and giving me eternal life. Make me the kind of person you want me to be.

The Christian Life

For the person who is a follower of Christ—a Christian—the penalty for sin is paid in full. But the effect of sin continues throughout our lives.

If we say we have no sin, we deceive ourselves, and the truth is not in us. (1 John 1:8)

For I do not do the good I want, but the evil I do not want is what I keep on doing. (Romans 7:19)

The effects of sin carry over into our marriages as well. Even Christians struggle to maintain solid, God-honoring marriages. Most couples eventually realize they can't do it on their own. But with God's help, they can succeed. To learn more, read the extended version of this article at FamilyLife.com/Resources.

leader's notes

What is the leader's job?

Your role is more of a facilitator than a teacher. A teacher usually does most of the talking and instructing whereas a facilitator encourages people to think and to discover what Scripture says. You should help group members feel comfortable and keep things moving forward.

Is there a structure to the sessions?

Yes, each session is composed of the following categories:

Warm-Up (5–10 minutes): The purpose of Warm-Up is to help people unwind from a busy day and get to know one another better. Typically the Warm-Up starts with an exercise that is fun but also introduces the topic of the session.

Blueprints (45–50 minutes): This is the heart of the study when people answer questions related to the topic of study and look to God's Word for understanding. Some of the questions are to be discussed between spouses and others with the whole group.

HomeBuilders Project (60 minutes): This project is the unique application that couples will work on between the group meetings. Each HomeBuilders project contains two sections: (1) On your own—questions for husbands and wives to answer individually and (2) With your spouse—an opportunity for couples to share their answers with each other and to make application in their lives.

In addition to these regular features, occasional activities are labeled "Picture This." These activities provide a more active or visual way to make a particular point. Be mindful that people have different learning styles. While most of what is presented in these sessions is verbal, a visual or physical exercise now and then helps engage more of the senses and appeals to people who learn best by seeing, touching, and doing.

What is the best setting and time schedule for this study?

This study is designed as a small-group, home Bible study. However, it can be adapted for more structured settings like a Sunday school class. Here are some suggestions for using this study in various settings:

In a small group

To create a friendly and comfortable atmosphere, we recommend you do this study in a home setting. In many cases the couple that leads the study also serves as host, but sometimes involving another couple as host is a good idea. Choose the option you believe will work best for your group, taking into account factors such as the number of couples participating and the location.

Each session is designed as a sixty-minute study, but we recommend a ninety-minute block of time to allow for more relaxed conversation and refreshments. Be sure to keep in mind one of the cardinal rules of a small group: good groups start *and* end on time. People's time is valuable, and your group will appreciate your respecting this.

In a Sunday school class

If you want to use the study in a class setting, you need to adapt it in two important ways: (1) You should focus on the content of the Blueprints section of each session. That is the heart of the session. (2) Many Sunday school classes use a teacher format instead of a small-group format. If this study is used in a class setting, the class should adapt to a small-group dynamic. This will involve an interactive, discussion-based format and may also require a class to break into multiple smaller groups.

What is the best size group?

We recommend from four to seven couples (including you and your spouse). If more people are interested than you can accommodate, consider asking someone to lead a second group. If you have a large group, you may find it beneficial to break into smaller subgroups on occasion. This helps you cover the material in a timely fashion and allows for optimum interaction and participation within the group.

What about refreshments?

Many groups choose to serve refreshments, which helps create an environment of fellowship. If you plan to include refreshments, here are a couple of suggestions: (1) For the first session (or two) you should provide the refreshments. Then involve the group by having people sign up to bring them on later dates. (2) Consider starting your group with a short time of informal fellowship and refreshments (15–20 minutes). Then move into the study. If couples are late, they miss only the food and don't disrupt the study. You may also want to have refreshments available again at the end of your meeting to encourage fellowship. But remember to respect the group members' time by ending the session on schedule and allowing anyone who needs to leave to do so gracefully.

What about child care?

Groups handle this differently, depending on their needs. Here are a couple of options you may want to consider:

- Have people be responsible for making their own arrangements.
- As a group, hire someone to provide child care, and have all the children watched in one location.

What about prayer?

An important part of a small group is prayer. However, as the leader, you need to be sensitive to people's comfort level with praying in front of others. Never call on people to pray aloud unless you know they are comfortable doing this. You can take creative approaches, such as modeling prayer, calling for volunteers, and letting people state their prayers in the form of finishing a sentence. A helpful tool in a group is a prayer list. You should lead the prayer time, but allow another couple to create, update, and distribute prayer lists as their ministry to the group.

Find additional help and suggestions for leading your Home-Builders group at FamilyLife.com/Resources.

about the leader's notes

The sessions in this study can be easily led without a lot of preparation time. However, accompanying Leader's Notes have been provided to assist you when needed. The categories within the Leader's Notes are as follows:

Objectives

The Objectives focus on the issues that will be presented in each session.

Notes and Tips

This section provides general ideas, helps, and suggestions about the session. You may want to create a checklist of things to include in each session.

Blueprints Commentary

This section contains notes that relate to the Blueprints questions. Not all Blueprints questions will have accompanying commentary notes. The number of the commentary note corresponds to the number of the question it relates to. (For example, the Leader's Notes, session 1, number 5 in the Blueprints Commentary section relates back to session 1, Blueprints, question 5.)

session one

the traps of adolescence

Objectives

Equipping your teenage children to avoid the traps of adolescence requires that you stay relationally connected with them.

In this session, parents will

- enjoy getting to know one another,
- examine some of the challenges of maintaining a close relationship with children as they enter the adolescent years,
- identify traps that can entice and lure teenagers into making foolish choices, and
- reflect on their need to pass on biblical convictions to their children.

Notes and Tips

1. Welcome to the first session of the HomeBuilders study *Guiding Your Teenagers*. In this first session, the focus should be on relaxing and making sure that everyone feels as comfortable as possible. A sense of comfort in the group will allow individuals to share serious issues more easily later in the study.

   As the leader, set a tone of openness by sharing on a

personal level. The degree to which you are open and willing to share during this course will have a direct impact on the level of sharing that occurs in the group.

2. If you haven't already done so, you'll want to read the information "About Leading a HomeBuilders Group" and "About the Leader's Notes" starting on page 105.

3. A great resource book for you—and to recommend to your group members—is *Parenting Today's Adolescent* by Dennis and Barbara Rainey. This book includes in-depth discussions of each of the traps of adolescence covered in this HomeBuilders study.

4. As part of the first session, you may want to review with the group some ground rules (see page ix in the introduction).

5. Although it's anticipated that the majority of participants in your group will be couples, you may also have single parents or one parent from a marriage represented. Regardless of the mix of people who participate, this course can be beneficial to all parents of teens and preteens. However, be aware that throughout this study you'll find certain features that are specifically designed for couples, such as designated couples questions and the Home-Builders projects.

   As the leader, be flexible and sensitive to your group. For example, if you have a single parent in your group, you might invite that person to join you and your spouse when a couples question is indicated in the study. Or, if there are multiple single parents, you may want to encourage them to join together for these questions. Likewise, for the HomeBuilders project at the end of every session, you may want to encourage singles to complete what they can individually or to work with another single parent on the project.

6. Throughout the sessions in this course, you'll find some questions that are designed for spouses to answer together. The purpose of these questions is to foster communication and unity between spouses and to give couples an opportunity to deal with personal issues. Although couples are free to share their responses to these questions with the group, be sensitive to the fact that not all couples will want to do so.

7. Before dismissing the group, make a special point to tell couples about the importance of the HomeBuilders project. Encourage them to make a date before the next meeting to complete this session's project. Mention that you'll ask about their experience with the project at the next session.

In addition to the HomeBuilders projects, there are six related Parent-Teen Interactions beginning on page 79. These are designed to help give parents an opportunity to communicate with their children. Though we recommend that parents try to complete the interactions between group sessions, we know that this will be a challenge. We encourage couples to place a priority on completing the HomeBuilders projects and then doing the Parent-Teen Interactions when they have time, whether between sessions or at a later date.

8. You may want to offer a closing prayer instead of asking others to pray aloud. Many people are uncomfortable praying in front of others, and unless you already know your group well, it may be wise to venture slowly into various methods of prayer. Regardless of how you decide to close, you should serve as a model.

Blueprints Commentary

Here is some additional information about various Blueprints questions. (Note: The following numbers correspond to the Blueprints questions they relate to.) If you share any of these points, be sure to do so in a manner that doesn't stifle discussion by making you the authority with the "right" answers. Begin your comments by saying things like, "One thing I notice in this passage is . . ." or "I think another reason for this is . . ."

2. Realize that there may be multiple solutions offered here. Be careful not to judge or criticize. The goal of this question is to spark interaction, not to seek agreement on one right approach or answer.
3. Most teenagers lack the maturity, basic life experience, and biblical convictions to make wise long-term decisions. By not grasping the lasting impact their decisions can have, and without the knowledge of certain consequences, teens can and often do make foolish mistakes. They are influenced by worldly philosophies they find in the media, and their peers often encourage them to engage in foolish and rebellious behavior.

Because of our sin nature, we all tend to act in foolish ways that expose us to unnecessary dangers, both physical and spiritual. The person given to folly tends to reject the limits or commands of God that have been given as an act of love and protection. This applies to parents as well as children, but teenagers are often placed in situations where this foolishness can have harsh consequences. For example:

- Speeding in an automobile without thinking about the dangers involved
- Experimenting with alcohol, drugs, or cigarettes because they think it won't hurt them to "just give it a try"
- Taking a drink or eating something at a party without asking what it is
- Hiding a mistake, a sin, or a foolhardy act from parents

4. Parents should fear God and keep his commandments. To teach their children about God and the Bible, parents need to be involved in different aspects of their lives so they have the freedom to talk about how to walk with God in each of those situations. Discussions about God and the Bible should permeate the conversations parents have with their children.

7. God's Word provides guidance for practically every decision we make in our lives, and "walking in the truth" means ordering your everyday life around biblical convictions.

9. By living out biblical convictions—taking an unpopular stand, refusing to compromise in public settings, calling the family to prayer—you can show your children that convictions based on the Word of God are more important than what people think or the consequences that may come. Through your example, your teen will know that believing God and the Word of God isn't only worth living for, but it's also worth dying for.

session two

peer pressure

Objectives

Your involvement in your teenager's life will help him or her exercise wisdom in choosing friends and resisting unhealthy influences from peers.

In this session, parents will

- discuss the influence peers have on adolescents,
- examine what the Bible says about the power of peer relationships, and
- share thoughts on how to stay involved in their teens' lives.

Notes and Tips

1. If new people come to this session, during Warm-Up ask them to share the names and ages of their children and why they decided to join the group.
2. If refreshments are planned for this session, make sure arrangements for them have been made.
3. If your group has decided to use a prayer list, make sure this is covered.
4. For this session's Warm-Up, you'll need to set up a mini obstacle course. You'll need six to eight sheets

of paper, a blindfold, and six to eight different "obstacles" (common, safe, unbreakable household items, books, chairs, plastic containers—whatever you have handy).

If you choose to let multiple people experience the obstacle course, you may spend longer than fifteen minutes on the Warm-Up section. If this happens, still try to finish the Blueprints section in thirty to forty minutes. It's a good idea to mark the questions in Blueprints that you want to be sure to cover. Encourage group members to look at any questions you don't get to during the session when they do the HomeBuilders project for the week.

5. If you told the group during the first session that you'd be asking them to share something they learned from the first HomeBuilders project, be sure to do so.

6. You may want to ask for a volunteer or two to close the session in prayer. Check ahead of time with a couple of people you think might be comfortable praying aloud.

7. ***Looking ahead:*** For the Warm-Up in session 3, you'll need to have copies of several popular magazines. Ideally these would be publications that you and members of your group subscribe to or read on a regular basis. Before you end this session, you may want to ask group members to bring a magazine with them to the next meeting. (It doesn't matter if the issue is current or old.)

Blueprints Commentary

3. A teen's peers often ridicule the standards and values you teach at home, and they encourage deceit and rebellion. As a result, teenagers stop listening to their parents at the very time when they need their guidance more than ever.

   Some examples of ways peers undermine parental authority include making fun of parents' rules, ridiculing teens who try to obey their parents, tempting other teens to reject parental authority, and encouraging their friends to lie to their parents.

4. Spending time with those who exhibit attitudes or behaviors that are rebellious toward God's Word can have a powerful influence on anyone—even teenagers with the best training at home. A well-behaved teenager may be influenced negatively by constant exposure to peers involved in wrong activities. Sometimes the association with "bad company" can begin innocuously—notice the progression in Psalm 1:1–3 from *walking with* the wicked, to *standing in* the company of sinners, and finally, to *sitting with* those who mock God.

5. Friends play a critical role in your child's spiritual maturity. Good friends can encourage teens to walk closely with God.

6. Parents may think that choosing friends happens naturally through common interests. Although that's often true, there are also children who will actively try to influence your teenager.

7. As we discussed in the previous session, teenagers will often make foolish choices. You must not give up the right to assist your teen in choosing friends and to determine who will have the strongest influence on him or her.

8. We all need emotional connections to other people. A child who is distant from parents will eventually seek to have emotional needs met in other ways. Peers will perform this role. This is one reason gangs are such a powerful influence on teenagers. They offer acceptance, relationships, and meaning to a drifting teen.

session three

sex

Objectives

You can help your teenagers avoid the trap of sex by challenging them to a high standard of purity and innocence.

In this session, parents will

- examine their convictions relating to sexuality and their teenagers,
- reflect on the preparation they have given—or need to give—their children to face the trap of sex as teenagers,
- look at what God's Word says about sex, and
- consider the influence the culture at large has on how teens view sex.

Notes and Tips

1. By this session, group members have probably warmed up a bit to one another but may not yet feel comfortable enough to open up and share on a deeper personal level. Don't force the issue. Continue to encourage everyone to attend and complete their projects.

2. For this session's Warm-Up, you'll need to have copies of several popular magazines (current or old issues). Women's, news, sports, entertainment, and health magazines

would all work well. Even better would be a selection of teen magazines.

For the breakout groups this Warm-Up calls for, you may want to consider creating subgroups of the same gender. This will provide an opportunity to see what, if any, differences there may be between how men and women assess what they consider to be inappropriate content.

Option: If you don't end up having copies of magazines for the Warm-Up, you could start the session this way: Say, "We live in a culture that's permeated with sex. If you turn on the television and watch regular network shows, it won't take long for you to hear sexual jokes, innuendos, and other sexually suggestive references." Then ask these questions:

- What philosophy do you think lies behind many of these messages?
- How do you think children are affected by these messages as they grow up?

3. Question 4 in Blueprints calls for couples to look up different Scripture passages. This approach allows for the group to simultaneously examine multiple scriptures. This saves time and gives the group a chance to learn from one another.

4. Congratulations! With the completion of this session, you'll be halfway through this study. It's time for a checkup: How's the group going? What has worked well

so far? What things might you consider changing as you approach the remaining sessions?

Blueprints Commentary

2. If we let our own past mistakes and sinful behavior prevent us from teaching our children the truth of God's Word, we would never feel free to teach them about anything.

3. If not properly taught, your children will learn about this vital aspect of life from peers or the world and will adopt those convictions. Their curiosity will drive them to find answers. Experimenting with the powerful emotional, physical, and spiritual bonding that occurs during sexual intimacy is like allowing children to play with matches and dynamite. Of course, in addition to the emotional scarring and guilt exists the danger of sickness or even death because of sexually transmitted diseases.

4. Genesis 1:27–28: Sex is for procreation in marriage.

    Genesis 2:22–25: God created sex.

    Proverbs 5:18–19: Sex is for intimacy and pleasure in marriage.

    Song of Solomon 2:2–7: Sexual passion is meant to be aroused and expressed in marriage.

    1 Corinthians 7:2–4: Sex is to be enjoyed by a man and woman in marriage.

    Hebrews 13:4: Sex outside marriage is sin.

5. God wants the best for us. Here are a few benefits of remaining pure until marriage—by waiting:

- You please God.
- You build trust, which is necessary for intimacy.
- You develop the God-honoring qualities of patience and self-control.
- You affirm that you care more for the other person than for yourself.
- You protect yourself from feelings of guilt and shame.
- You provide yourself with an example to give your children.
- You're protected from emotional, mental, and physical trauma should you break off your relationship.
- You develop healthy communication habits and skills.
- You avoid the possibility of an unwanted pregnancy.
- You maintain a clear conscience before God and man.
- You increase the anticipation and enjoyment of your wedding night.
- You experience the blessing of obedience.
- You discover more about each other than just the physical.
- You maintain a witness to a lost world.
- You keep from bringing reproach on the name of Christ.

6. Suggested follow-up question: In what ways, if any, do you think responses would differ between Christian and non-Christian parents?

7. This is a growing view among teens; in recent years there has been an upswing of teens who engage in oral sex but don't think of it as sex because it doesn't involve sexual intercourse. This type of "technical virginity" still

violates God's commands against sexual immorality. It's also dangerous because some diseases can be transmitted even without engaging in sexual intercourse.

8. When it comes to sex, the Bible gives us a higher goal to set for our children than virginity. The goal of instructing our children should be to help protect their purity and innocence. These two God-given gifts are lost long before intercourse if a teen begins to experience the sexual response that God designed for marriage. We must set our sights high and challenge our teenagers to the highest standard—God's standard. As parents, we should want our children to arrive at marriage innocent of evil, pure in their sexuality, and with a healthy view of marriage—not encumbered by a lot of emotional baggage from past sexual mistakes.

Keeping your children "innocent as to what is evil" (Romans 16:19) means trying to keep them from experiencing evil as much as you can. In today's culture, absolute innocence is impossible, of course. But it is possible to limit the amount of exposure and experience a child has.

9. Protecting the innocence of children involves at least three things: (1) you must model purity in your own behavior, (2) you must set clear standards for your children in the area of sexual morality, and (3) you must challenge your children to these standards and continue to stay in touch with them to see how they're holding to them. This can mean some uncomfortable conversations and questions, such as, "Where are you drawing the line when you go out on a date?"

session four

dating

Objectives

One of your greatest challenges as a parent is to set solid dating standards for your teen.

In this session, parents will

- discuss the nature and practice of dating in today's culture,
- reflect on their responsibility to set standards for their teens, and
- look at and discuss scriptures related to the key issues surrounding dating.

Notes and Tips

1. As the leader of a HomeBuilders group, one of the best things you can do is pray specifically for each group member. Take time to pray as you prepare for this session.
2. Remember the importance of starting and ending sessions on time.
3. By this time, group members should be getting more comfortable with one another. For prayer at the end of this session, you may want to give anyone an opportunity to pray by asking the group to finish a sentence that

starts something like this: *"Lord, I want to thank you for
_____."* Be sensitive to those who may not be comfort-
able doing this.

4. You may want to make some notes right after the meeting to help evaluate how things went. Ask yourself questions, such as, Did everyone participate? Is there anyone
I should make a special effort to follow up with before
the next session? Asking yourself questions like these
will help you focus.

Blueprints Commentary

1. Some of the reasons the dating game, as currently played
by most people, can be a dangerous trap for teenagers are:

- One-on-one dating leads couples to spend too much
time alone at the peak of the sex drive for a young
man.
- Teens make poor choices about whom to date and are
negatively influenced by those who don't share their
values.
- Teens develop premature emotional attachments with
the opposite sex.
- These emotional attachments cause them to desire a
physical relationship of the same intensity.
- Acting either from peer pressure or from a need that
isn't being met at home, teens begin pairing off as
boyfriend and girlfriend when they're too young and
immature to make good decisions.

2. Our popular media depicts a type of "fantasy love" in which young people look to fulfill their romantic dreams and fantasies—and think nothing of dropping one relationship to pursue that fantasy with another person. It portrays an unbiblical view of sex; physical intimacy between unmarried couples is shown so continually that it's easy for teenagers to assume it should be a normal part of a dating relationship. It also encourages people to view marriage entirely within the context of personal fulfillment rather than unconditional commitment.

3. If a young person spends too much time in the emotionally and physically volatile environment of a relationship with the opposite sex, personal growth will be affected. Most of the time a teenager isn't able to understand how emotional attachments form and then lead to some type of physical expression. Early attachments serve no real positive purpose in a culture where most people don't select a spouse and marry until their twenties. Too much emphasis on early pairing off also robs children of other necessary and rewarding opportunities to develop their interests and social skills. And it leaves them vulnerable to succumbing to sexual temptation at an early age. Finally, the pattern some teens have of moving from one boyfriend or girlfriend to another may lay the groundwork for restlessness and discontentment later in marriage.

4. Key convictions or character qualities include learning how to treat the opposite sex with honor; how to avoid compromising situations; how to maintain physical,

emotional, and spiritual purity; and how to be accountable to parents.

8. This Scripture passage is often cited as a reason why a Christian shouldn't marry a non-Christian. But teenagers should also understand why it's not a good idea to seek any kind of romantic relationship with "unbelievers." If a teen enters into a relationship with an unbeliever, he or she runs a great risk of sliding away from a close relationship with God. Parents should help their teenagers evaluate their dating relationships. Not every person who uses the label "Christian" is sincere about his or her faith and is seeking to grow in Christ. A teenager caught up in emotions may not be able to exercise this level of discernment about another person without a parent's loving, gentle assistance.

session five

media

Objectives

Teenagers need to develop discernment about the type and amount of media they consume.

In this session, parents will

- think about and discuss the way media impacts family life,
- evaluate media on both a time and content basis, and
- consider media standards from a biblical perspective.

Notes and Tips

1. You and your spouse may want to consider writing notes of thanks and encouragement to the members of your group this week. Thank them for their commitment and contribution to the group, and let them know that you are praying for them. Make a point to pray for them as you write their notes.

2. In this session, be prepared for differences in opinion on the quality and influence of various types of television shows, music, movies, and so forth. You may find that some group members have few standards about media, while others are very strict. Encourage the group to inter-

act without an attitude of judgment. The greatest value of this type of discussion may be in how it challenges us as parents to evaluate the impact of media and set standards.

3. **Looking ahead:** For the next session—the last session of this study—you may want to ask an individual or a couple to share what this study or group has meant to them. If you want to do this, think about the person or couple you'll ask to share.

Blueprints Commentary

1. Many adolescents haven't learned how to make good choices about media and lack discernment about good and bad messages. Many take their cues on how to dress and cut their hair, what to eat and drink, what music to listen to, what people to look up to, and so much more, from the media. The media messages our preteens and teenagers allow themselves to hear and see will sink deep into their minds and will affect their attitudes and behavior.

3. One of the biggest problems with media is that people let it take up too much of their time. In families it can prevent deep relationships from being built. Passive media consumption can also lead to an unhealthy desire to be entertained. You could say that our entire culture is overly obsessed with entertainment.

4. Ask people to give specific examples of what they've seen or heard in current movies, TV shows, or songs.

5. Often media will encourage us to do or believe things that are contrary to God's Word. Media influence such

things as the importance we place upon material possessions, how we relate to other people, what we believe about the purpose and place of sexual intimacy, and more. Popular forms of media often ridicule biblical morality and feeds our selfish nature.

8. One approach to this question is to ask what kinds of things are true, honorable, just, pure, lovely, commendable, excellent, or praiseworthy. Then ask, How can we focus on these good things while partaking of all the media choices we're offered?

session six

substance abuse

Objectives

Your connectedness with your teen, your integrity, and your walk with God will help your child deal with one of the deadliest traps of adolescence.

In this session, parents will

- consider the consequences that teens and their families face from substance abuse,
- discuss selected passages of Scripture in relation to substance abuse, and
- close this course by discussing the need for them and their children to have a strong personal relationship with God.

Notes and Tips

1. Some group members may be threatened by this session's topic because of past experiences they haven't shared with others, so be sensitive to those who seem hesitant to talk.

2. Blueprints question 7 in this session gives people in the group an opportunity to share about their personal relationship with God. Before the next meeting you may

want to consider asking a couple of people in the group to briefly share what God has done in their lives. Choose people who you know would be comfortable answering this question.

3. Although this HomeBuilders study has great value, people are likely to return to previous patterns of living unless they commit to a plan for carrying on the progress they've made. During this final session of the course, encourage couples to take specific steps beyond this series to continue to build their homes. For example, you may want to challenge couples who have developed the habit of a "date night" during this study to continue this practice. You may also want to discuss doing another HomeBuilders study.

4. Here's a suggestion for making the closing prayer time of this last session special: Have the group form a prayer circle. Then have each individual or couple, if they're comfortable doing so, take a turn standing or kneeling in the middle of the circle while the group prays specifically for them.

5. As a part of this session, you may want to devote some time to planning one more meeting—a party to celebrate the completion of this study!

Blueprints Commentary

1. Reasons for experimentation include the influence of TV and movies, rebellion, stress, curiosity, an inability to stand up to peer pressure, a desire to experiment with

"grown-up" behaviors, a cry for help, and escape from reality.

2. These substances are damaging to the body: They can damage the brain, cause addiction and death, lead to other more dangerous life choices, and often destroy family relationships.

First Corinthians 6:19–20 tells us that our bodies are not our own. As a Christian, you have the Holy Spirit dwelling in you. When Jesus died on the cross, God purchased you, setting you free from the control and destruction of sin. The battle within us is to yield to the Spirit so we don't give our bodies over to destructive things.

5. Our example as parents is the first source for behavior and conviction that our children have. Without a firm foundation in a relationship with us, it will be much more difficult for our teens to take a stand when facing temptations from peers or another group.

7. If you sense that not everyone in the group understands what it means to have a relationship with Christ, recommend for further reading the article "Our Problems, God's Answers" (page 97).

8. Temptations and ideas will be presented to your teens that they won't be able to resist without the power and presence of God in their lives. In the final analysis, a relationship with Jesus Christ is the only reason to remain pure and undefiled by harmful substances.

9. Some truths that can be gleaned from this passage: Be obedient. Faithfully keep the commands of God

and teach them to your children. Don't be like those who have rejected God's commands. Avoid stubbornness and rebelliousness toward God. Be a loyal follower of God.

more tools for leaders

Looking for more ways to help people build their marriages and families?

Thank you for your efforts to help people develop their marriages and families using biblical principles. We recognize the influence that one person—or couple—can have on another, and we'd like to help you multiply your ministry.

FamilyLife is pleased to offer a wide range of resources in various formats. Visit us online at FamilyLife.com, where you will find information about our:

- getaways and events, featuring Weekend to Remember, offered in cities throughout the United States;
- multimedia resources for small groups, churches, and community networking;
- interactive products for parents, couples, small-group leaders, and one-to-one mentors; and
- assortment of blogs, forums, and other online connections.

who is familylife?

FamilyLife is a nonprofit, Christian organization focused on the mission of helping every home become a godly home. Believing that family is the foundation of society, FamilyLife works in more than a hundred countries around the world to build healthier marriages and families through marriage getaways and events, small-group curriculum, *FamilyLife Today* radio broadcasts, Hope for Orphans® orphan care ministry, the Internet, and a wide range of marriage and family resources.

about the authors

Dennis Rainey is the president and a cofounder of FamilyLife (a ministry of Campus Crusade for Christ) and a graduate of Dallas Theological Seminary. For more than thirty-five years, he has been speaking and writing on marriage and family issues. Since 1976, he has overseen the development of FamilyLife's numerous outreaches, including the popular Weekend to Remember marriage getaway. He is also the daily host of the nationally syndicated radio program *FamilyLife Today*. Barbara is an artist and author. Her books include *Thanksgiving: A Time to Remember, Barbara and Susan's Guide to the Empty Nest,* and *When Christmas Came.* The Raineys have six children and eighteen grandchildren.